W9-AKE-484

Chesterfield County Public Library
9501 Lori Road
Chesterfield, VA 23832

Kathryn Heling and Deborah Hembrook

Clothesline Clues to Sports People Play

Illustrated by Andy Robert Davies

Charlesbridge

For my siblings: Kristine, Karl, Tricia, and Amy. It's always fun hanging out together!—K. E. H.

To my nephew, Logan. Love from your #1 fan!—D. K. H.

For my son, Henry.—A. R. D.

Text copyright © 2015 by Kathryn Heling and Deborah Hembrook
Illustrations copyright © 2015 by Andy Robert Davies
All rights reserved, including the right of reproduction in whole or in part in any form.
Charlesbridge and colophon are registered trademarks of Charlesbridge Publishing, Inc.

Published by Charlesbridge, 85 Main Street, Watertown, MA 02472
(617) 926-0329 • www.charlesbridge.com

Library of Congress Cataloging-in-Publication Data
Heling, Kathryn, author.
Clothesline clues to sports people play/Kathryn Heling and Deborah Hembrook;
illustrated by Andy Robert Davies.
  pages cm
  ISBN 978-1-58089-602-3 (reinforced for library use)
  ISBN 978-1-60734-861-0 (ebook)
  ISBN 978-1-60734-862-7 (ebook pdf)
1. Sports—Juvenile literature. 2. Sports uniform—Juvenile literature.
3. Sporting goods—Juvenile literature. I. Hembrook, Deborah, author.
II. Davies, Andy Robert, illustrator. III. Title.
GV749.U53H45 2015
796.028'4—dc23   2014010490

Printed in China
(hc) 10 9 8 7 6 5 4 3 2 1

Illustrations done in pencil and mixed media, manipulated digitally
Display type and text type set in Jesterday
Color separations by Colourscan Print Co Pte Ltd, Singapore
Printed by C & C Offset Printing Co. Ltd. in Shenzhen, Guangdong, China
Production supervision by Brian G. Walker
Designed by Susan Mallory Sherman and Whitney Leader-Picone

High on the clotheslines
the clues swing and sway.
Who uses these things
for the sports that they play?

Catcher's mitt and bat,
a uniform in gray.
Cap, ball, and bases.
What sport does he play?

He plays baseball.

Team shirt, goalie gloves.
A ball to kick away.
Long socks and shin guards.
What sport does she play?

She plays soccer.

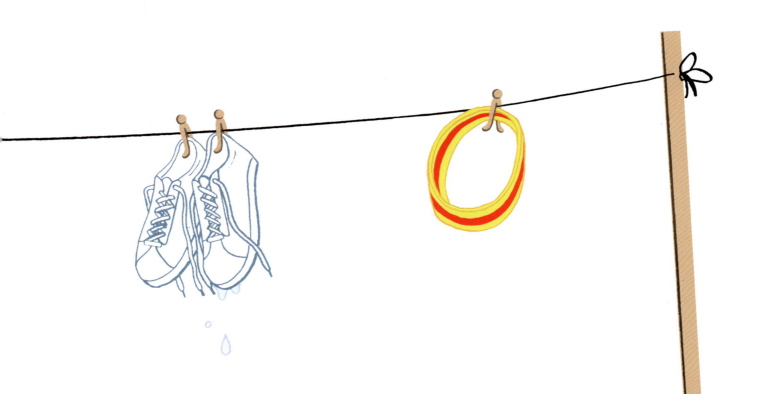

A racquet and fuzzy balls
for practice time today.
Sneakers and sweat band.
What sport does she play?

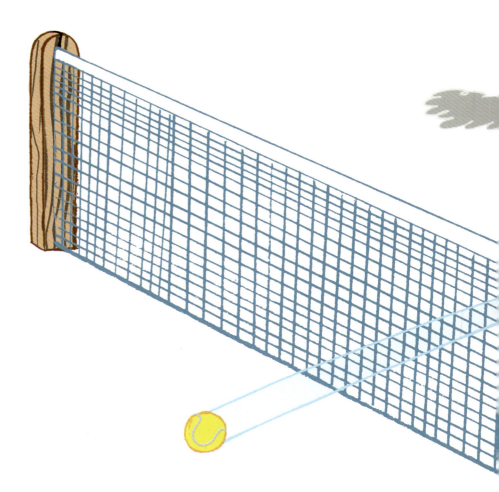

She plays tennis.

A sword called a foil.
Opponents make way!
Mask, gloves, and jacket.
What sport does he play?

He does fencing.

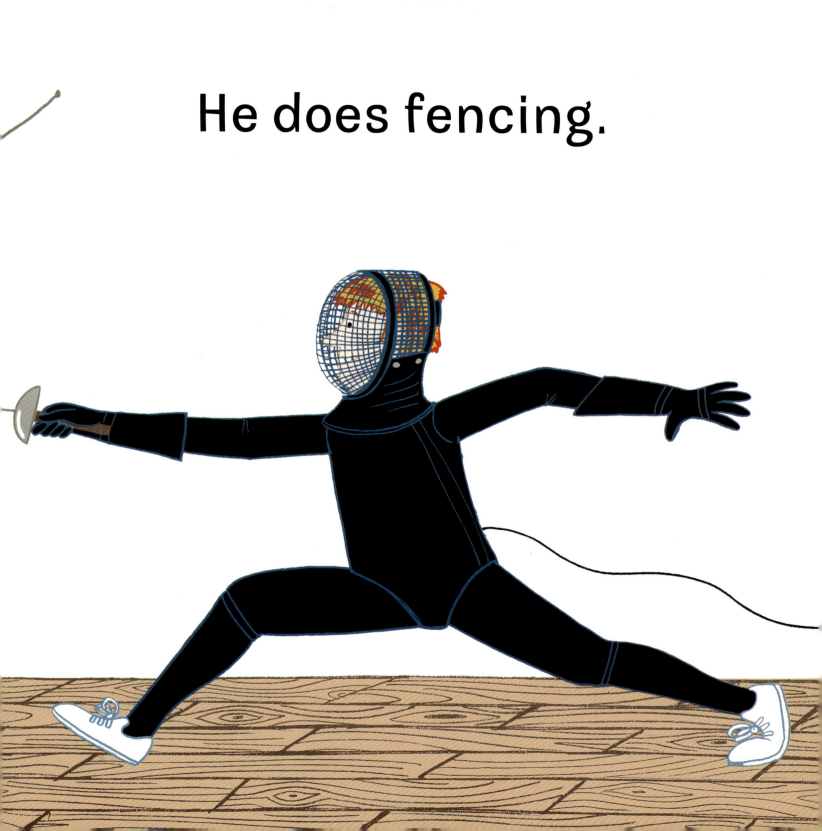

High-tops, orange ball.
Score two points—hooray!
Gym shorts and tank top.
What sport does she play?

She plays basketball.

Helmet and shoulder pads,
strap them on to stay.
Jersey and leather ball.
What sport does he play?

He plays football.

Bow, arrows, and quiver.
A target on display.
Fitted shirt and arm guard.
What sport does she play?

She does archery.

The clotheslines hold clues
to sports people play.
What sport would you like
to try out today?

MAY MSN (2015)